Foxes

Sneaky Rascals

Dr. Richard A. NeSmith

Love of Nature Series

ISSUE 5

Applied Principles of Education & Learning

APE-Learning   http://richardnesmith.obior.cc

© **2020 Richard A. NeSmith**
Love of Nature Series

Dr. Richard A. NeSmith

dr.nesmith@gmail.com

Oct. 2021

ISBN: 9798667023883

FLESCH-KINCAID GRADE LEVEL: 8.2

Foxes
(*Vulpes* and *Urocyon cinereoargenteus*)

Foxes are usually shy and cautious animals. They are very *cunning* (sneaky) and have excellent reasoning abilities.

Because of their sly and crafty nature, these creatures were the incentive for the popularity of the 1600 A.D. British fox hunts' origin. Foxes often outsmarted specialized hunting dogs.

There are six species of foxes, all members of the dog family (Canidae). These include the arctic fox, grey fox, kit fox, island fox, and red fox. Male foxes are called "dogs" or "dog fox," while females are called "vixens." Offspring, baby foxes are called "kits," or cubs, or pups. Red foxes weigh from 10-15 pounds and can be up to 2 feet long, with a bushy tail measuring 1 foot itself.

All are omnivores and have 46 well-developed canine teeth. Like their cousin the dog, they are susceptible to numerous diseases and parasites, including rabies. Rabies is a contagious and fatal viral disease of dogs and other mammals that causes madness and convulsions and is transmissible through the saliva to humans. Symptoms include fearfulness, aggression, excessive drooling, difficulty swallowing, staggering, paralysis, and seizures.

Avoid being bitten by a rabid animal. If you see an animal you suspect has rabies, call your county health department or animal control agency.

Foxes are bushy-tailed dogs with long fur, pointed ears (which they can rotate 150 degrees), and a narrow snout.

They come in various colored hues of red, rust, silver-black, white, and cross). The red foxes have black stockings on the legs, black tips on the ears, and scattered along the tail. Their chest, belly, and throat are light-brown to white.

This book's focus will be on the red fox, the genus species,

Some foxes have been domesticated as household pets.

Vulpe *vulpes*, with some differences between the gray fox (*Urocyon cinereoargenteus*) mentioned. The confusing aspect is that the gray fox can also have a lot of reddish fur, while the red fox can, at times, have a lot of grayish hair. To clearly identify and differentiate these two, we will leave that to the professionals.

Range

There are more than 7.2 million red foxes throughout most

of the US continental mainland. Usually regarded as strictly territorial animals, red foxes inhabit different and well-separated ranges from one another. These predators' home ranges can vary in size up to 20 square miles (30 km). Red foxes are one of the most common and widespread fox species in the world. They live around the world in many diverse habitats, including forests, grasslands, mountains, and deserts, as well as in neglected citrus groves, pine, and oak woods. They even live in Australia as an *introduced* species in the 1870s. Most red foxes live to be three years in the wild, with the average age in captivity being 10-12 years.

Red foxes are considered native (endemic) throughout most of the United States and are successful and prolific in most regions. Their success is probably because of being

very well-adapted to human environments, such as farms, suburban areas, and even large communities. Though they prefer to live in more dense, inaccessible cover, foxes tend to tolerate more human disturbance than many other mammals. Like the bobcat, they can be elusive. Still, they have been known to birth kits in some of the most unusual and unexpected locations. One such hiding place included the faux ceiling of a house. This event happened where a vixen gave birth and raised her pups in a fake "drop-down" ceiling. Other den accommodations included: under the floorboards of a classroom and in a vacant, dilapidated, abandoned building.

Characteristics

Most foxes are nonviolent and avoid conflicts with other animals. Though they will consume livestock such as chickens, that is not a common practice, for the foxes prefer to live in wilder, more dense brushy cover. Though possibly a learned behavior based on food scarcity, they can become a nuisance under such conditions. Like any wild

beast, if their space is invaded and there is no apparent

escape route, they will defend themselves and their young. Otherwise, a healthy fox is no danger to humans.

Diet

Red foxes are *solitary hunters*. The majority of their diet consists of small invertebrates, small mammals, and plants, including tubers, grasses, acorns, and sedges (a grass-like plant with triangular stems growing in wet soil). However, their favorite plants include fruits, such as cherries, persimmons, mulberries, blueberries, grapes, plums, apples, raspberries, and blackberries. Invertebrates include insects, mollusks, earthworms, and crayfish. Vertebrate prey includes frogs, toads, small reptiles, fish, songbirds, eggs, mice, rats, rabbits, or hares. The red and gray fox both serve to help maintain a balance in the rodent and rabbit populations. They significantly reduce the number of ducks in midcontinent areas and pheasants in the Great Basin region of the USA. The cottontail and marsh rabbits make up the *largest* part of a fox's diet. Foxes tend to eat up to 1 to 2 pounds (.05 to 1 kg) of food each day.

They possess an acute (accentuated) sense of hearing. They can locate small animals in thick grasses and bushes and then jump high in the air to pounce on them unawares.

They can quietly stalk prey, keeping themselves hidden until close enough to dash in and catch the animal by surprise. As with most canines, foxes are incredibly possessive of their food and do not share with others. If the kill is plentiful, they will attempt to reserve the extra underground for a later time.

Predators of red foxes include eagles, owls, hawks, coyotes, bobcats, gray wolves, bears, mountain lions, dogs, and humans. Especially the young pups are vulnerable. Many foxes die annually from hunting or become automobile roadkill.

Habitat

Foxes seem to prefer living along the edges of forests, in tilled fields, and near marshes. Female foxes, especially when needing to deliver little pups, often prefer an underground den. However, foxes tend to be less fussy about the types of places they use as underground den sites than other animals. Foxes dig about 50 percent of the burrow holes they use for their dens. Dens can also be hollow logs, gopher holes, or hollow trees. A preferred den site tends to be sheltered (among trees, under buildings, or dense vegetation such as a thorny bush or prickly shrubs). Or on well-drained soil (often sloped) with loose, easily burrowed soil. A foxes' den (**lair**) is usually 20-40 feet long and has more than one entrance. The den is relatively

simple but sometimes an elaborate complex maze, with a hollowed-out chamber at the end of the entrance tunnel where the fox sleeps and where cubs are raised. The compartments are typically between 3 to 10 feet (1-3 meters) below ground, with tunnels typically leading to more than one opening (the main entrance and emergency exit). One biologist noted nearly all of the dens were on southeast-facing slopes and had an average inclination (angle) of 20-30 degrees.

Dens, possibly only utilized when raising offspring, have been rather unhygienic, even causing other mammal housemates to leave the premises. Though, the use of these as winter quarters is not uncommon. It is suspected that the fox's digging may alter the natural composition of flora (plant and vegetation), soil fertility, pH, and changing the types of plants due to dormant seeds on their coats and passed through their feces.

By the age of seven months, foxes, particularly males, tend to prefer being left-hand or right-handed, at least in the direction in which they curl up on the ground during periods of resting (called the *resting side*). It appears that these resting states of rest provide some means by which a fox can lower its breathing to as little as one breath every 25 seconds (compared to humans or dogs, who breathe approximately once every 6 seconds). Such lowering of the metabolism results in requiring less food than other animals with less efficient respiratory systems.

The gray fox is widespread across most of the United States except northern plains and Rockies. While found

throughout the Southeastern United States, it is less abundant in southern Florida. Generally found in wooded areas, as it prefers to live in more inaccessible thick cover

Here, one can see the slits in the fox's eyes, similar to that of a cat's.

types of forests.

Behavior

Red and gray foxes are primarily nocturnal and very agile, alert, and fast. It does occasionally feed during the day. It can run 30 mph (48 kph) for short distances. They can climb trees to escape predators, rest, and pursue prey. Unlike gray foxes (and cats), however, red foxes don't have much rotation in their forearms and cannot climb trees in the same manner. Gray foxes can grasp both sides of the trunk with their rotational forearms and retractable claws and then push up with their hind legs. This difference limits the red fox to trees with low branches on which they can jump. Red foxes can *lunge* six feet up in the air. Regardless,

foxes will often climb trees to search for food (birds, eggs, fruit, etc.), escape flooding, or rest in the sunshine, but in rare cases, they have been known even to make homes in trees.

Reproduction

Foxes tend to link up with a mating partner for life. Mating occurs during late winter or early spring, producing a litter of 1-7 pups 53 days later. Kits are born helpless, brownish-black in color, blind, and their eyes open on the 9th day following birth. They nurse for nearly two months. Then, they stay with the *vixen* in the den while the *dog* helps bring food for the next 5 to 6 weeks. The kits/pups grow rapidly but remain with their parents until they are seven months old, under the mother's protection and defense. After about eight months, the pups move off to be on their own to establish their territory and secure a mate.

Miscellaneous

A group of foxes is called a skulk or leash. Their pupils are vertical, similar to a cat, helping them see well at night or under dim light conditions. Also, like the cat, the fox has sensitive whiskers and spines on its tongue. It walks on its toes, which accounts for its elegant, cat-like tread. Foxes

have excellent hearing. Red foxes can, reportedly, hear a mouse squeak over one hundred yards away. Foxes are not very pleasant-smelling animals to humans. To us, they stink, with an odd 'musky' smell coming from scent glands at the base of their tail.

Foxes may be known to be *sneaky*, but they can also be friendly and curious. They tend to play amongst themselves, and other animals, such as cats and dogs do. They love balls, which they will steal from backyards and golf courses.

Another peculiar characteristic regarding foxes is the ability to utilize the Earth's magnetic field. Foxes seem to be able to detect the Earth's magnetism. They have whiskers on their legs and face, which help them to navigate. Few other animals have this *magnetic sense* honing ability. Some birds, sharks, and turtles do. But, the fox is the first discovered to use it to catch prey.

It was found that foxes aligned their bodies in a northeasterly direction. As a result, the hit rate reached an astounding 73% success rate versus the average 18% success rate. In addition, aligning to the Earth's magnetic field enabled them to be 50% more accurate during a "mouse pounce." According to *New Scientist*, the fox can "see" the Earth's magnetic field as a *ring of shadow* on its eyes that darkens as it heads towards the magnetic north. When the prey's shadow aligns with the prey's sound, then the fox pounces accurately. Scientists continue to study this phenomenon. This orientation permits the fox to align with its prey more accurately and then accurately pounce on it.

Though red and gray foxes are not as abundant as raccoons, they are not far behind their growing population. They are intelligent, curious, and *sly*. Sly as a "fox"! They have the reputation of *outfoxing* hunting dogs and being *sneaky rascals*. Usually, they are not a menace or a threat to humans. They may not be as elusive as the bobcat, but they keep their distance and need us to respect their space. One

thing everyone can agree on, they are *cute as buttons*, especially the pups.

If you have the opportunity to see one in the forest, stop and admire it. Don't approach or try to pet or feed it. Just

watch it. It will be very curious about you and what you are doing. Keep your distance, and you will be safe, and in a short time, the fox will be off on his or her way for their next adventure. If you see one, you will never forget it. And, you will know you were given another special honor that only nature can bestow upon you. Respect it as a wild animal, and bestow upon it your *love of nature.*

REVIEW

1. **What is the Genus *species* is the red fox?**

2. **Where are red and gray foxes found in the United States?**

3. **How did red foxes end up on the island continent of Australia?**

4. **What three things do you remember about the red fox and its digging of a den?**

5. **What is unique about the red fox's eyes, and why?**

6. **What are male foxes and female foxes called?**

7. **How high can a fox leap up in the air?**

8. **Why would a fox catch and kill a chicken?**

9. **Why do you think the vixen might prefer an underground den?**

FOX

COLORING PAGE

http://www.supercoloring.com/coloring-pages/red-fox-2

Name:_________________

Foxes: Sneaky Rascals

Carefully read each statement and complete the crossword puzzle by inserting the correct word into the proper location.

Created using the Crossword Maker on TheTeachersCorner.net

slit   navigate   Foxes   trees   ducks   rabies   rabbit   vixen   teeth   solitary   dog

canine   frequency   miles   dens   dogs   introduced   lair

Across

1. The average range/territory size of a fox is 20 square_________.
5. Type of teeth foxes have?
8. Foxes are able to hear very well and can even hear low-________?
10. Foxes most likely dinner meal will be that of a _____
12. Foxes have 46 of these?
14. Foxes use a 'magnetic field' to _______?
15. Used to hunt foxes during special hunting parties?
16. The red fox has ______ eyes.

Down

2. Type of hunter a fox is?
3. Animals in this book include the red and gray _______.
4. Another name for a 'den.'
6. Which animal/prey does the fox seem to keep in check regarding their population?
7. Term for when an animal was brought to an area and released?
9. Name for a female fox?
11. Like dogs and most mammals, foxes are susceptible to _____?
12. Foxes are able to climb _____?
13. Underground holes used to raise pups in?
15. Name for a male fox?

INTERESTING SOURCES TO CONSIDER

16 Amazing Fox Species. Available at: https://youtu.be/XUqjCbjbCxo

Discover useful facts about the FOX. Available at:
https://youtu.be/1Hm0Ep-Ae2c

Fox Facts for Children. Available at: https://youtu.be/4_zEiHhvqF0

Hike & Seek: Red Foxes & Coyotes. Available at:
https://youtu.be/lCo2btlr_Cg

How foxes use magnetic fields to catch prey - The Wonder of Animals: Episode 5 Preview - BBC Four. Available at:
https://youtu.be/1MWoPKlAXx4

National Geographic: Red Fox. Available at:
https://www.nationalgeographic.com/animals/mammals/r/red-fox/

National Geographic: The Secret Life of Fox - Wildlife Wars. Available at: https://youtu.be/utvVUNrn5X8

National Wildlife Federation: Red Fox. Available at:
https://www.nwf.org/educational-resources/wildlife-guide/mammals/red-fox

Red Fox Facts. Available at: https://youtu.be/QfZ0T--zRZY

Red Fox in The Wild - Newborn Kits to Adults. Available at:
https://youtu.be/30YGRZN8kO4

Red Fox Information, Photos, and Facts. American Expedition. Available at: https://forum.americanexpedition.us/red-fox-facts-information-and-photos

Red Fox. Animal Diversity Web. Available at:
https://animaldiversity.org/accounts/Vulpes_vulpes/

Red Fox. Britannica. Available at:
https://www.britannica.com/animal/red-fox-mammal

Red Fox: *Vulpes vulpes*. Nature Works. Available at:
http://www.nhptv.org/natureworks/redfox.htm

Red Foxes. Colorado Parks and Wildlife. Available at:
https://cpw.state.co.us/fox

The Red Fox: Natural History and Wildlife Biology. Available at:
https://youtu.be/x34eQBEioXk

ABOUT THE AUTHOR

Richard NeSmith is a native of Florida, USA. He grew up wading through the swamps of central Florida with his two younger brothers during the pre-Disney era and unknowingly, falling in love with biology, wildlife, and nature. He has lived in seven American states, twice in Australia and once in Mexico City. He holds eight university degrees and has taught for 14 years in secondary schools, here and abroad, and another 13 years as professor in several American universities. His service includes professor of science education, Dean of Education, Campus Dean, and an online instructor. His passion for learning (and *how we learn*) did not develop until *after* graduating from high school. His only explanation for this is that *having a goal made all the difference in the world*. He enjoys reading, hiking, nature photography, golf, and tennis.

Educational, wildlife, and naturalist books
Dr. Richard NeSmith.

Applied Principles of Education & Learning

APE-Learning

Available on Amazon.com at
http://amazon.com/author/richardnesmith

Applied Principles of Education & Learning presents

AMAZON AUTHOR's PAGE:

https://www.amazon.com/author/richardnesmith

e-books: **https://bit.ly/3iuCgB3**

Issue 1
Raccoons:
Friendly Bandits
Dr. Richard NeSmith

Issue 2
Sandhill Cranes
&
Pileated Woodpeckers
Flaming Redheads
Dr. Richard NeSmith

Issue 3
American
Alligators
&
Crocodiles
Dr. Richard NeSmith

Issue 4
Bobcats:
Ghostly Elusive
Dr. Richard NeSmith

Issue 5
Foxes:
Sneaky Rascals
Dr. Richard NeSmith

Issue 6
Armadillo:
Little Armored One
Dr. Richard NeSmith

Issue 7
Squirrels:
Bushy Tail Scampers
Dr. Richard NeSmith

Issue 8
River Otters:
Aquatic Clowns!
Dr. Richard NeSmith

Issue 9
Beavers:
Nature's Engineers!
Dr. Richard NeSmith

Issue 10
Black Bears
Titans of the Forest
Dr. Richard NeSmith

Issue 11
Freshwater
Turtles
Dr. Richard NeSmith

Issue 12
FUNGI, LICHENS
& MUSHROOMS
Dr. Richard NeSmith

NEW: *Love of Nature* Series ISSUES 1-10 in a single volume! $ave 50% off
363-pages/ enhanced / full-color

https://bit.ly/2Y8k7DV

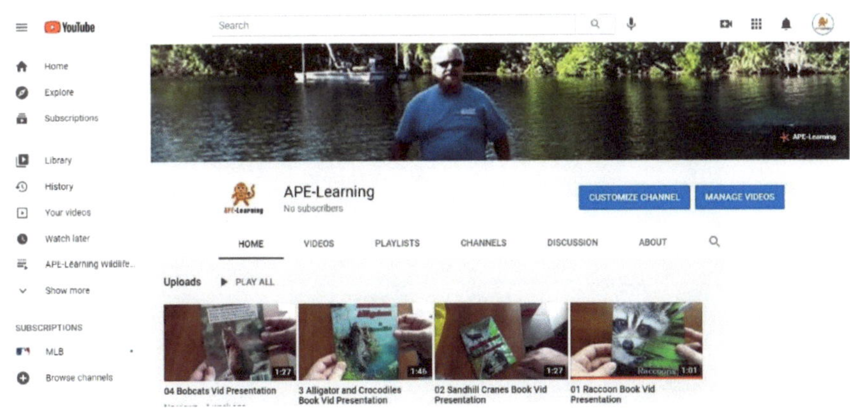

[i] Special thanks to the following who kindly provided permission to use their photographs on pixaby.com: David Mark, rottonara, Ad Adriaans, skeeze, Tom Frydenlund, Alain Audet, Pexels, and Barbor Marisol). Thank you to Sunyu on Unsplash) In addition, special thanks to **Ken Buckley**, **Kori Stolte DeSio**, and **Brenda Phillips-Bely**. And, as always, special thanks to **Dr. Laurie Aleixo**, for her relief work, her photographs, and her support and encouragement. Finally, *a special thank you to **Stacey Diamond** for her wonderful photograph used to create the book cover.* **Thank you all.**

Learning – Love Nature – Love Life